Summer Key

TO TREES OF TENNESSEE AND THE GREAT SMOKIES

Royal E. Shanks and Aaron J. Sharp
University of Tennessee, Knoxville

The key and accompanying list include the trees known to be native or naturalized in Tennessee. Species known to occur in the Great Smoky Mountains National Park are indicated by an asterisk (*) before the name. Certain species not native to the region, some of which escape from cultivation, are included but are so designated by CAPITALS. The present key is an expansion of the "Summer Key to the Trees of Eastern Tennessee" by the same authors, *Jour. Tenn. Acad. Sci.* 22:114–133, 1947, which was based on ten years of experience with the key prepared by Stanley A. Cain in 1937, for use in introductory botany classes at the University of Tennessee. It is in many places a recognizable descendant of Cain's key and the obligation is acknowledged with sincere appreciation.

The key is based on summer characters, primarily those of leaves, the most important of which are defined on pages 22 to 24 and illustrated on the inside covers. The illustrations were prepared by Jane W. Roller. At times the identification of a species is facilitated by the use of flower, fruit, bud, leafscar, habit, and habitat characters, but they are usually not required. The key is artificial, no attempt having been made to reveal phylogenetic relationships.

For winter identification of most of these trees see the "Winter Key to the Trees of Eastern Tennessee," by Billings, Cain, and Drew, *Castanea* 3:29–44, 1937.

SUMMER KEY TO TREES OF TENNESSEE AND THE GREAT SMOKIES is Contribution New Series No. 124 from the Department of Botany, The University of Tennessee/Copyright 1950 by R.E. Shanks and A.J. Sharp.

Published 1963 by The University of Tennessee Press.
Second printing 1965.
Third printing 1966.
Fourth printing 1968.
Fifth printing 1972.
Sixth printing 1980.
Seventh printing 1988.
Eighth printing 1991.
Ninth printing 1997.
Tenth printing 2008.

KEY TO GENERA

Keys to the species within the genera will be found in the alphabetical list of genera which follows this key. When a genus includes only one arborescent species within the area, the full name is included in the key to genera.

1. Deciduous trees (leaves of one year falling before the sub-
   sequent leaves expand 3
1. Evergreen trees (leaves persisting into the second year or
   longer; leaves broad, hard, leathery, or needle-like or scale-
   like) 2
   2. Trees with needle-like leaves or small scale-like leaves ....
   .... Group A
   2. Trees with broad, hard, leathery leaves........................ Group B
3. Thorn-bearing trees; branches and sometimes trunks bearing
   various kinds of thorns..................................... Group C
3. Trees without thorns.. 4
   4. Trees with two or more leaves at a node..................... Group D
   4. Trees with alternate leaves (leaves, leaf-scars, lateral
   branches, and buds characteristically one at a node)................... 5
5. Leaves compound.. Group E
5. Leaves simple, sometimes deeply lobed but never with distinct leaflets... Group F

Group A

Key to the genera with needle or scale-like leaves

1. Leaves needle-like, 2, 3, or 5 in a bundle with a sheath at
   the base, 5 to several cm. long.................................... *Pinus*
1. Leaves not in bundles, linear or scale-like, less than 5 cm.
   long 2
   2. Leaves all small, scale-like, overlapping, the leafy twig
   more or less flattened... 3
   2. Leaves not all small and scale-like, not on flattened
   twigs... 4
3. Leaves of 2 shapes, the lateral ones overlapping the edges
   of the decidedly flattened twigs...
   ....*Thuja occidentalis* L. (Northern white cedar)
3. Leaves nearly uniform, on slightly flattened branchlets
   which often curve at the tips. .... CHAMAECYPARIS
   4. Leaves produced more or less in one plane.......................... 9
   4. Leaves spreading in all directions, at least on young
   growth 5
5. Leaves flattened.. 7
5. Leaves 4-angled, square in cross section............................... 6

6. Leaves 2–5 cm. long, clustered on very short branches......... CEDRUS
6. Leaves less than 2 cm. long, uniformly distributed along the
branches... .... *Picea*
7. Leaves awl-shaped, tapering to a sharp point, or scale-like.... .. ..
....:.............*Juniperus virginiana* L. (Red cedar)
7. Leaves linear.. 8
8. Leaves borne on stalks, which persist on the twigs after the
leaves have fallen; cones pendent...... ....
.........................*Tsuga caroliniana* Engelm. (Carolina hemlock)
8. Leaf stalks not persisting on twigs; cones erect..................... .*Abies*
9. Leaves borne on stalks which persist on the twigs after the
leaves have fallen; cones pendent................. .. ..
.... *Tsuga canadensis* (L.) Carr. (Eastern hemlock)
9. Leaf stalks not persisting on twigs; cones erect..... ....
.... *Abies fraseri* (Pursh) Poir. (Southern balsam fir)

Group B

Key to the genera of broad-leaf evergreens

1. Leaf margins undulate, all with a few stout spinose teeth.. ....
.... *Ilex opaca* Ait. (American holly)
1. Leaf margins entire or with small teeth... 2
2. Leaf margins crenate-serrulate and ciliate................. .. ..
.... *Pieris floribunda* (Pursh) B. & H. (Rosemary, fetterbush)
2. Leaf margins not ciliate.............................. 3
3. Leaves obovate to oblong, usually less than 4 cm. in length: fruit
a berry........ *Vaccinium arboreum* Marsh. (Farkleberry, winter huckleberry)
3. Leaves averaging more than 5 cm.; fruit not a berry.......... 4
4. Twigs encircled by a stipule scar at each node: fruit a cone.... .. .
.... *Magnolia*
4. Twigs not encircled by stipule scars.... 5
5. Leaf blades averaging more than one dm. long... . ... *Rhododendron*
5. Leaf blades averaging less than one dm. long...... 6
6. Leaf margins revolute; leaves oblanceolate, occasionally lobed:
fruit an acorn; typically a tree.... ....
.... QUERCUS VIRGINIANA Mill. (Live oak)
6. Leaf margins not revolute; leaves ovate-lanceolate to oblong;
fruit a capsule; typically a shrub............................ .
.... *Kalmia latifolia* L. (Mountain laurel)

Group C

Key to the genera of trees with thorns on the stem

1. Leaves simple.. 5
1. Leaves compound...................................... 2

2. Leaves at least in part decompound (more than once pinnate). 4
2. Leaves all pinnately compound (once pinnate)................... 3
3. Leaflets ovate, rounded at both ends, not punctate................ .. *Robinia*
3. Leaflets ovate, pointed, glandular-punctate...............................
.... *Xanthoxylum americanum* Mill. (Prickly ash)
   4. Leaves very large (6-12 dm. long) bi- to tripinnate, borne in a
   cluster at the top of the stem; thorns simple........ ....
   ... . *Aralia spinosa* L. (Devil's walking stick)
   4. Leaves smaller (less than 3 dm. long), pinnate to bipinnate,
   scattered on the twigs; thorns stout, frequently branched...............
   .... *Gleditsia*
5. Leaves entire... 7
5. Leaves variously toothed, sometimes lobed............................ 6
   6. Twigs typically stout, over 3 mm. in diameter; the spur branches
   which are prolonged into thorns but little differentiated and often
   bearing leaves; leaves not deeply lobed.......................... *Pyrus*
   6. Twigs typically slender, less than 3 mm. in diameter; thorns differentiated, stiff and sharp; leaves often deeply lobed............. *Crataegus*
7. Petioles 2-5 cm. long; leaves acuminate, usually rounded at the
base; the multiple fruit spherical, 10-15 cm. in diameter..................
.... MACLURA POMIFERA (Raf.) Schneid. (Osage orange)
7. Petioles 1-2 cm. long; leaves acute to rounded at the apex, tapering
at the base; fruit a cherry-like drupe.........................
.... *Bumelia lycioides* (L.) Gaertn. (Buckthorn bumelia)

Group D

Key to the genera with 2 or more leaves at a node

1. Leaves simple......... 4
1. Leaves compound.. 2
   2. Leaves palmately compound (leaflets clustered at the apex of
   the petiole)...................................... *Aesculus*
   2. Leaves pinnately compound or trifoliate... 3
3. Leaflets 3 to 5, coarsely toothed toward the apex; fruit double-
winged..................................... *Acer negundo* L. (Boxelder)
3. Leaflets commonly 7-11, entire or finely toothed; fruit single-
winged... *Fraxinus*
   4. Leaves characteristically whorled (3 at a node)................... *Catalpa*
   4. Leaves characteristically opposite, seldom whorled.................... 5
5. Leaves heart-shaped, large (1.5-3 dm. long); exotic tree of city
plantings, frequently escaped...
.... *PAULOWNIA TOMENTOSA (Thunb.) Steud. (Empress tree)
5. Leaves not heart-shaped, smaller............................. 6
   6. Leaves entire or toothed, but not lobed............................· 8
   6. Leaves both toothed and lobed.................................... 7
7. Twigs velvety........................... ....
.... *BROUSSONETIA PAPYRIFERA (L.) Vent. (Paper mulberry)
7. Twigs not velvety... *Acer*

8. Leaves obscurely to strongly serrate or crenulate..................... 12
8. Leaves strictly entire...... 9
9. Leaves less than 5 cm. long, ovate to elliptic; escaped shrub
occasionally attaining tree form....... LIGUSTRUM VULGARE L. (Privet)
9. Leaves more than 5 cm. long; native.............................. 10
  10. Leaf-blades typically oblong, 8–24 cm. long; buds with several exposed scales; stipules absent................................
  .... *Chionanthus virginicus L. (Fringe tree)
  10. Leaf-blades ovate to elliptic, seldom more than 10 cm. long;
  vegetative buds elongate, with 2 valvate scales............ 11
11. Leaves acute to rounded at tip, with somewhat revolute margin,
frequently stipulate.... ....
.... Viburnum nudum L. (Large withe-rod, possum-haw viburnum)
11. Leaves typically acuminate at tip; lateral veins strongly incurving toward leaf tip; stipules absent...................... .... Cornus
  12. Twigs velvety................................ ....
  .... *BROUSSONETIA PAPYRIFERA (L.) Vent. (Paper mulberry)
  12. Twigs not velvety................. 13
13. Leaves distinctly serrate................... .... Viburnum
13. Leaves obscurely serrate or crenulate toward the apex.... 14
  14. Leaves broadly ovate, crenulate; primary veins arising from
  the lower two-thirds of the midvein, strongly incurving; trees
  of uplands..................... *Cornus florida L. (Flowering dogwood)
  14. Leaves oblong-ovate or ovate-lanceolate, obscurely serrate;
  veins pinnate throughout; shrubby trees of river swamps.. ....
  .... Forestiera acuminata (Michx.) Poir. (Swamp privet)

Group E

Key to the genera with alternate compound leaves

1. Leaves pinnately compound (once pinnate).... 4
1. Leaves decompound (more than once-pinnate)....... 2
  2. Upper pinnae undivided (merely toothed), lower pinnae divided; all apices acuminate; fruit a drupe........................ ......
  .... *MELIA AZEDARACH L. (Chinaberry)
  2. All pinnae divided into pinnules; fruit a legume (pod)... 3
3. Leaflets oval, about 5 pairs to each pinna; pod large, heavy
(1–2.5 dm. long); pith orange or salmon-colored.. ....
.... Gymnocladus dioica (L.) K. Koch (Kentucky coffee-tree)
3. Leaflets one-sided, about 20–25 pairs to each pinna; pod flat;
thin (.5–1 dm. long); pith white...............................
.... *ALBIZZIA JULIBRISSIN Duraz. (Mimosa)
  4. Leaves with glands on lower teeth, often with offensive odor
  when crushed... ....
  .... *AILANTHUS ALTISSIMA (Mill.) Swingle (Tree-of-heaven)
  4. Leaves without such glands.. 5
5. Leaves with odor of green walnuts when crushed, pith chambered
.... Juglans
5. Leaves without walnut odor, pith not chambered........................ 6

6. Leaves without pulvini; fruit not a legume......................... 8
6. Leaves with pulvini; fruit a legume............................... 7
7. Leaflets all opposite.. *Robinia*
7. Leaflets mostly alternate..
.... *Cladrastis lutea* (Michx. f.) K. Koch (Yellowwood)
8. Stipules or stipule scars present; buds red; vein scars 3 or 5.
.... *Sorbus americana* Marsh. (Mountain ash)
8. Stipules absent; buds not red; vein scars more numerous............. 9
9. Lateral buds partially or wholly concealed by petioles; fruit a
small dry drupe; pith large....................................... *Rhus*
9. Lateral buds not concealed by petioles; fruit a nut, husk
splitting along 4 lines; pith small, angled........................... *Carya*

Group F

Key to the genera with alternate simple leaves

1. Leaves needle-like, 1–1.5 cm. long, 2-ranked on deciduous
branchlets............................ *Taxodium distichum* Rich. (Bald cypress)
1. Leaves not needle-like... 2
2. Leaves fan-shaped, more or less incised or divided at the
broad summit; veins dichotomous; leaves alternate but partly
clustered on spur branches...... GINKGO BILOBA L. (Maiden-hair tree)
2. Leaves not fan-shaped; net-veined............................... 3
3. Leaves variously toothed or lobed or both............................ 13
3. Leaves strictly entire (never more than gently undulate)................. 4
4. Leaves heart-shaped.................... *Cercis canadensis* L. (Redbud)
4. Leaves not heart-shaped...................................... 5
5. Leaves mostly less than 1.5 dm. long............................... 7
5. Leaves mostly more than 2 dm. long............................... 6
6. Twigs encircled by a stipular scar at each node................. *Magnolia*
6. Without stipules.................. *Asimina triloba* (L.) Dunal (Pawpaw)
7. Leaves characteristically clustered at tips of twigs with very
short internodes; pith 5-angled; fruit an acorn..................... *Quercus*
7. Internodes not markedly shortened at branch tips; only one leaf
at tip of each elongate vegetative branch; pith cylindrical or
nearly so; fruit a drupe or berry.................................. 8
8. Leaves obovate to orbicular, usually rounded at apex.................
.... *Cotinus obovatus* Raf. (Smoke tree)
8. Leaves acute or acuminate at apex.............................. 9
9. Leaves with the upper 2 lateral veins strongly incurving.................
.... *Cornus alternifolia* L. (Blue dogwood, alternate-leaved dogwood)
9. Leaves pinnately veined to the tip................................. 10
10. Twigs and leaves spicy-aromatic................................
.... *Lindera benzoin* (L.) Blume (Spicebush)
10. Twigs and leaves not spicy-aromatic............................ 11
11. Leaves leathery, sweet to taste; often obscurely toothed.................
.... *Symplocos tinctoria* (L.) L'Her. (Sweetleaf, horse sugar)
11. Leaves neither leathery in texture nor sweet........................ 12

12. Pith diaphragmed but solid, vein scars 3 . . . . *Nyssa*

12. Pith sometimes with cavities but not diaphragmed; vein
scar one . . . . *Diospyros virginiana* L. (Persimmon)

13. Leaf-blade usually averaging at least 1.5 times as long as
broad 23

13. Leaf-blade usually about as broad as long 14

14. Leaves more or less regularly toothed, but not lobed 19

14. Leaves usually with a few conspicuous lobes, toothed or
entire 15

15. Leaves bilaterally and symmetrically lobed 17

15. Some leaves unlobed, others asymmetrically lobed 16

16. Leaves coarsely serrate; fruit a multiple "berry" 21

16. Leaves not serrate; fruit a drupe . . . .
. . . . *Sassafras albidum* (Mitt.) Nees (Sassafras)

17. Leaf-tip truncate or broadly notched; leaves with one pair of
broad, acute, lateral lobes . . . .
. . . . *Liriodendron tulipifera* L. (Tulip tree, yellow poplar)

17. Leaf-tip acuminate; leaves with main veins and lobes essen-
tially palmate 18

18. Leaves star-shaped with deep notches between lobes,
margin with fine, regular serrations . . . .
. . . . *Liquidambar styraciflua* L. (Sweet gum)

18. Leaves not star-shaped, with shallow sinuses; margins
entire except for a few sinuate teeth . . . .
. . . . *Platanus occidentalis* L. (Sycamore)

19. Leaf margins merely undulate or crenate; axillary buds stalked . . . .
. . . . *Hamamelis virginiana* L. (Witch hazel)

19. Leaf margins distinctly toothed; buds not stalked 20

20. Leaves all unlobed in our species, smooth above; sap not
milky 22

20. Trees usually with some irregularly lobed leaves but occasionally all unlobed; leaves usually somewhat harsh
above; sap milky; fruit multiple 21

21. Leaves velvety on lower surface, bases oblique, petioles 5–10
cm. long; twigs velvety . . . .
. . . . *BROUSSONETIA PAPYRIFERA* (L.) Vent. (Paper mulberry)

21. Leaves not velvety, usually not oblique, petioles 2–4 cm. long;
twigs not velvety . . . . *Morus*

22. Leaves in 2 rows; pith cylindrical . . . . *Tilia*

22. Leaves in more than 2 rows; pith 5-angled . . . . *Populus*

23. Leaves characteristically clustered at tips of twigs, with
very short internodes, prominently lobed or coarsely and
regularly toothed; pith 5-angled; fruit an acorn . . . . *Quercus*

23. Leaves not characteristically clustered at tips except on
spur branches; if somewhat clustered, with glandular petioles;
if somewhat lobed, less than 8 cm. long; pith cylindrical;
fruit not an acorn 24

24. Sap milky; fruit multiple and fleshy; leaves ovate to
cordate . . . . occasional forms of *Morus*

24. Sap not milky; fruit not multiple and fleshy; leaves ovate
    to lanceolate.. 25
25. Teeth of leaf-margins bristle-tipped............................. *Castanea*
25. Teeth of leaf-margins not bristle-tipped........................ 26
  26. Leaves in 2 rows, more or less in one plane.................. 27
  26. Leaves in more than 2 rows.................................. 35
27. Leaves with 2 prominent lateral veins from base of blade;
    lateral buds appressed; pith typically chambered.............. *Celtis·*
27. Leaves otherwise; pith continuous.............................. 28
  28. Leaves with main lateral veins dissipating into smaller
      veins before reaching the margin; fruit a small pome (apple-
      like); buds long and tapering............................. *Amelanchier*
  28. Main lateral veins extending into teeth of leaf margin; fruit
      not a pome... 29
29. Terminal bud long and tapering, at least 4 times as long as
    broad; leaves coarsely serrate; fruit a bur with two triangular
    nuts... *Fagus*
29. Terminal buds less than 4 times as long as broad; leaves
    finely or doubly serrate..................................... 30
  30. Most leaves bilaterally symmetrical or nearly so............ 32
  30. Most leaves decidedly lop-sided, especially at base......... 31
31. Leaf margins mostly doubly serrate, not glandular............. *Ulmus*
31. Leaf margins singly serrate, teeth glandular.................
    .... *Planera aquatica* (Walt.) Gmel. (Planer tree, water elm)
  32. Trunk and larger branches smooth, with fluted or projecting
      ridges, "muscular" in appearance; bud-scales in 4 rows.............
      .... **Carpinus caroliniana* Walt. (Blue beech)
  32. Trunk and larger branches without fluted or projecting
      ridges... 33
33. Some lateral veins forked; bark longitudinally shredded; len-
    ticels inconspicuous; fruit completely enclosed in a papery
    sac..................... **Ostrya virginiana* (Mill.) K. Koch (Hop hornbeam)
33. Lateral veins unforked and continuous to leaf margin.......... 34
  34. Bark relatively smooth except in very old trees; lenticels
      conspicuous, laterally elongated on larger branches and
      trunk; fruit winged, in cone-like clusters................. *Betula*
  34. Bark ridged or scaly; lenticels inconspicuous; fruit a
      samara... *Ulmus*
35. Leaf-blades less than 4 times as long as broad................ 37
35. Leaf-blades at least 4 times as long as broad................. 36
  36. Bud with one exposed scale................................. *Salix*
  36. Bud with about 6 exposed scales............................ *Prunus*
37. Buds distinctly stalked; fruit a woody cone-like structure.........
    .... **Alnus serrulata* (Ait.) Willd. (Alder)
37. Buds not stalked; fruit otherwise............................. 38
  38. Stipules or stipular scars present......................... 43
  38. Neither stipules nor stipular scars present................ 39
39. Leaves leathery, sweet to taste; often obscurely toothed..........
    .... *Symplocos tinctoria* (L.) L'Her. (Sweetleaf, horse sugar)
39. Leaves neither leathery in texture nor sweet................. 40

40. Leaves distinctly sour to taste, margins ciliate; twigs
    greenish-red . . . . *Oxydendrum arboreum* (L.) DC. (Sourwood)
40. Leaves not sour; twigs brown or dark gray 41
41. Twigs rusty-tomentose with persistent hairs; leaf-margins
    closely and sharply serrate . . . . *Clethra acuminata* Michx. (White alder)
41. Twigs not tomentose; hairs, if present, scattered; leaf-
    margins not both closely and sharply serrate 42
    42. Buds hairy, without scales; flowers axillary and solitary . . . .
        . . . . *Stewartia ovata* (Cav.) Weatherby (Mountain stewartia)
    42. Buds glabrous, covered with scales; flowers in clusters . . . .
        . . . . *Halesia carolina* L. (Silverbell)
43. Petioles with one or more glands near the blade; fruit a drupe . . . . *Prunus*
43. Petioles without glands 44
    44. Wood of twigs yellowish and ill-smelling; leaves obscurely
        toothed, with main lateral veins ending in margin . . . .
        . . . . *Rhamnus caroliniana* Walt. (Carolina buckthorn)
    44. Wood of twigs neither yellowish nor ill-smelling; leaves
        distinctly toothed with main lateral veins not extending to
        leaf-margin 45
45. Vein-scar one . . . . *Ilex*
45. Vein-scars two or more 46
    46. Younger twigs averaging less than 3 mm. in diameter; leaves
        finely and regularly serrate . . . . *Amelanchier*
    46. Younger twigs averaging more than 3 mm. in diameter; leaves
        coarsely toothed or irregularly lobed . . . . *Pyrus*

ALPHABETICAL LIST OF GENERA WITH KEYS TO SPECIES

Abies fraseri (Pursh) Poir. (Southern balsam fir)

Acer

1. Leaves compound . . . . *A. negundo* L. (Boxelder)
1. Leaves simple 2
    2. Buds with 4-8 scales apparent, essentially sessile; flowers
       in lateral clusters; trees of various habitats 4
    2. Buds with 2 valvate scales, distinctly stalked; flowers in
       terminal racemes; small trees of high mountains 3
3. Twigs and buds glabrous; leaves finely serrate, with 3 main
   veins; bark striped with whitish lines . . . .
   . . . . *A. pensylvanicum* L. (Striped maple)
3. Twigs and buds pubescent; leaves coarsely serrate, with 5
   main veins; bark not striped . . . . *A. spicatum* Lam. (Mountain maple)
    4. Leaves usually with 7 prominent veins from petiole; leaf-
       scars meeting; sap milky when evident; exotic trees fre-
       quent in city planting . . . . A. PLATANOIDES L. (Norway maple)
    4. Leaves with 3 or 5 prominent veins from petiole; leaf-
       scars usually not meeting; sap not milky; native trees 5
5. Buds ovoid, flower buds rounded and collaterally multiple,
   usually 4 scales showing 8
5. Buds conical, exposed scales 6 or more 6

    6. Leaves averaging less than 8 cm. wide; small tree with
      chalky-white bark, reported in Tennessee only from south-
      eastern corner. . . . . *A. leucoderme* Small (Chalk maple)
    6. Leaves averaging more than 8 cm. wide; larger trees with
      grayish-brown bark. 7
  7. Leaves not yellow-green beneath, not drooping at margins;
    buds smooth; twigs buff. . . . . *A. saccharum* Marsh. (Sugar maple)
  7. Leaves yellow-green beneath, drooping at margins; buds
    hairy; frequently with foliaceous stipules. . . . .
    . . . . *A. nigrum* Michx. f. (Black maple)
    8. Lobes of leaves narrowed at the base; twigs ill-smelling;
      bark flaking. . . . . *A. saccharinum* L. (Silver maple, water maple)
    8. Lobes of leaves not narrowed at the base; twigs not ill-
      smelling; bark tight, not flaking. 9
  9. Leaves 3-lobed; twigs and lower leaf surface usually pubes-
    cent; leaves conspicuously paler beneath. . . . .
          A. rubrum var. *trilobum* K. Kock (Carolina red maple)
  9. Leaves usually 5-lobed, lower pair small. 10
    10. Twigs and leaves glabrous at maturity or nearly so; fruit
      usually 2–3.5 cm. long. . . . . *A. rubrum* L. (red maple)
    10. Twigs more or less pubescent at maturity; leaves with a
      dense, usually persistent tomentum below; fruit usually
      4–5 cm. long. . . . .
      . . . . . *A. rubrum* var. *drummondii* (H. & A.) Sarg. (Drummond red maple)

Aesculus
    1. Buds gummy-resinous; leaves coarse, veiny; leaflets often
      7. . . . . A. HIPPOCASTANUM L. (European horse-chestnut)
    1. Buds not gummy; leaves thinner and less veiny; leaflets 5. 2
      2. Fruit warty; leaflets reaching 15 cm. in length; stamens
        exserted; small tree of lowlands. . . . . *A. glabra* Willd. (Ohio buckeye)
      2. Fruit smooth; leaflets reaching 20 cm. in length; stamens
        included; large tree of the mountains. . . . .
      . . . . *A. octandra* Marsh. (Yellow buckeye)

*AILANTHUS ALTISSIMA (Mill.) Swingle (Tree of heaven)

*ALBIZZIA JULIBRISSIN Duraz. (Mimosa)

Alnus serrulata (Ait.) Willd. (Alder)

Amelanchier
    1. Leaves glabrous below; young leaves brownish-green. . . . .
    . . . . *A. laevis* Wiegand (Service berry)
    1. Leaves pubescent below; young leaves whitish-green. . . . .
    . . . . *A. arborea* (Michx. f.) Fern. (Shadbush)

Aralia spinosa L. (Devil's walking stick, Hercules' club)

Asimina triloba (L.) Dunal (Pawpaw)

Betula
1. Twigs with odor of wintergreen.................................... 2
1. Twigs without odor of wintergreen................................. 3
  2. Bark on young trees and branches peeling, yellowish;
    . cone bracts ciliate; leaves cuneate or slightly heart-
    shaped at base.. ....
    .... *B. lutea* Michx. *(B. alleghaniensis* Britt.) (Yellow birch)
  2. Bark on young trees and branches cherry-like, tight; cone
    bracts glabrous; leaves heart-shaped or rounded at base..... .. ..
    .... *B. lenta* L. (Sweet birch)
  3. Bark white; leaves cordate in part, margins rather coarsely
    serrate or doubly serrate............................... .. ..
    .... B. PAPYRIFERA var. CORDIFOLIA (Regel.) Fern. (Paper birch)
  3. Bark red-brown; leaves with a broadly wedge-shaped base,
    conspicuously doubly serrate................ . *B. nigra* L. (River birch)

*BROUSSONETIA PAPYRIFERA (L.) Vent. (Paper mulberry)

Bumelia lycioides (L.) Pers. (Buckthorn bumelia)

**Carpinus caroliniana* Walt. (Blue beech)

Carya
1. Buds with more than 6 overlapping scales; leaflets 3-9,
   the uppermost largest..................................... . 4
1. Buds with 4-6 scales in pairs, meeting at edges; leaflets
   7-17, usually lanceolate, often curved... 2
  2. Leaflets 9-17; nut cylindric, longer than broad, shell
    thin, smooth; bark with flat, scaly, interlacing ridges....... ....
    .... *C. illinoensis* (Wang.) K. Koch (Pecan)
  2. Leaflets 7-13; nut somewhat flattened, about as broad
    as long, kernel bitter................... 3
  3. Leaflets 7-9; buds yellow, with elongate scales; shell of
    nut smooth and thin........... ....
            C. cordiformis (Wang.) K. Koch (Bitternut hickory)
  3. Leaflets 7-13; buds reddish brown; shell of nut irregularly
    angular; restricted to river swamps and stream banks.... ....
    .... *C. aquatica* (Michx. f.) Britton (Water hickory)
    4. Larger terminal buds over 12 mm. in length.. 5
    4. Terminal buds smaller (less than 10 mm.)........ 7
  5. Twigs buff or orange-colored, glabrous; nut at least 3 cm.
    long, shell thick; bark splitting off in long strips; leaflets
    7-9; typically in bottomlands or along streams.....................
    .... *C. laciniosa* (Michx. f.) Loud. (Big shellbark hickory)
  5. Twigs brown or gray, often somewhat pubescent; nut and
    bark various; typically on uplands................... 6
    6. Twigs red-brown to gray with age; leaflets typically 5,
    terminal leaflet stalked; bark splitting off in long strips.............
    .... **C. ovata* (Mill.) K. Koch (Shagbark hickory)

6. Twigs bright-brown to gray; leaflets typically 7-9,
stellate-pubescent; terminal leaflet sessile or nearly
so; bark tight . . . .   *C. tomentosa* Nutt. (Mockernut hickory)
7. Leaflets typically 7 9
7. Leaflets typically 5 8
8. Bark tight, hard, light gray; fruit pear-shaped; twigs and
buds chestnut-colored . . . .   *C. glabra* (Mill.) Sweet (Pignut hickory)
8. Bark splitting off in strips; fruit nearly spherical with thick
hull; buds black; leaflets lanceolate, especially the lower
ones . . . .   *C. carolinae-*
septentrionalis (Ashe) Engl. & Graebn. (Carolina hickory)
9. Leaf rachis and veins densely woolly with fascicled hairs,
when young silvery with peltate scales; buds and fruits
yellowish with granular scales . . . .
. . . .   *C. pallida* (Ashe) Engl. & Graebn. (Sand hickory)
9. Leaves typically glabrous at maturity, finely serrate, never
scurfy or glandular; fruit thin-hulled . . . .
. . . .   *C. ovalis* (Wang.) Sarg. (Red hickory)

Castanea

1. Leaves glabrous beneath; more than one nut in a bur; a large
tree, most specimens of which are dead or dying . . . .
. . . .   *C. dentata* (Marsh.) Børkh. (Chestnut)
1. Leaves tomentose beneath; nut only one in a bur; a small
tree seldom over 2 dm. in diameter . . . .
. . . .   *C. pumila* (L.) Mill. (Chinquapin)

Catalpa

1. Leaves rarely angled, with unpleasant odor when bruised;
bark thin, flaky; lower lobes of corolla entire; pods about 8
mm. broad; seeds pointed . . . .   C. BIGNONIOIDES Walt. (Catalpa)
1. Leaves often angled, without unpleasant odor; bark thick
and rough; lower lobe of corolla notched at apex; pods fully
10 mm. broad; seeds obliquely truncate . . . .
. . . .   *C. speciosa* Warder (Western catalpa)

CEDRUS DEODARA Loud. (Deodar cedar)

Celtis

1. Leaf-blades seldom more than 5 cm. in length; fruit dark
orange-red, on stalks about as long as the petioles; small
tree . . . .   *C. tenuifolia* var.
georgiana (Small) Fern. & Schub. (Georgia hackberry)
1. Leaf-blades usually more than 5 cm. in length; fruit on
stalks longer than the petioles; becoming large trees 2
2. Leaf-blades entire, or toothed toward the apex; bark
light gray, with corky warts . . . .
. . . .   *C. laevigata* Willd. (Sugarberry, southern hackberry)
2. Leaf-blades strongly toothed to well below the middle 3

3. Leaves tending to be lanceolate, blades tapering at both
   ends; buds about 3 mm. long; bark light gray with corky
   warts, even on older trees...
   .... *C. laevigata var. smallii Sarg. (Small's sugarberry, hackberry)
3. Leaves tending to be ovate, rounded or subcordate at base;
   buds about 6 mm. long; bark warty on branches, ridged on
   trunks of older trees.................... *C. occidentalis L. (Hackberry)

*Cercis canadensis L. (Redbud)

CHAMAECYPARIS sp. (White cedar)

*Chionanthus virginicus L. (Fringetree)

*Cladrastis lutea (Michx. f.) K. Koch (Yellowwood)

*Clethra acuminata Michx. (White alder)

Cornus
1. Leaves irregularly alternate; fruit blue.............................
   .... *C. alternifolia L. f. (Blue dogwood, alternate-leaved dogwood)
1. Leaves always opposite... 2
   2. Leaves broadly ovate, with 5-6 pairs of lateral veins;
      twigs with appressed hairs, usually glaucous; flower
      clusters with 4 large petal-like bracts; fruit red, in dense
      heads......................... *C. florida L. (Flowering dogwood)
   2. Leaves ovate, with 3-4 pairs of lateral veins; flowers
      without petal-like bracts; fruit blue or white, in loose
      cymes 3
3. Leaves rough above, woolly pubescent beneath; twigs
   grayish or light brown; fruit white.................................
   .... C. drummondi C. A. Meyer (Roughleaf dogwood)
3. Leaves glabrous; twigs reddish-brown; fruit pale blue.................
   .... C. foemina Mill. (C. stricta Lam.) (Stiff dogwood)

Cotinus obovatus Raf. (Smoke tree)

*Crataegus (Hawthorn, red haw)
   Forty-seven species of this difficult and confused genus
   have been credited to Tennessee. Flower and fruit characters are required for identification and no key is here at-
   tempted.

*Diospyros virginiana L. (Persimmon)

Fagus
1. Leaves with 9-14 pairs of veins, serrate............................
   .... *F. grandifolia Ehrh. (American beech)
1. Leaves with 5-9 pairs of veins, denticulate.........................
   .... F. SYLVATICA L. (European beech)

Forestiera acuminata (Michx.) Poir. (Swamp privet)

Fraxinus
1. Twigs 4-angled, or 4-winged; buds gray . . . .
. . . . *F. quadrangulata* Michx. (Blue ash)
1. Twigs round in cross-section, at least not prominently angled 2
   2. Leaflets elliptic-oval, conspicuously whitened beneath,
     entire or obscurely serrate 3
   2. Leaflets not conspicuously whitened beneath, often serrate 4
3. Twigs and leaves glabrous . . . . *F. americana* L. (White ash)
3. Twigs pubescent; leaves more or less pubescent . . . .
. . . . *F. americana* var. *biltmoreana* (Beadle) J. Wright (Biltmore ash)
   4. Twigs and leaves glabrous . . . .
. . . . *F. pennsylvanica* var. *subintegerrima* (Vahl) Fern. (Green ash)
   4. Twigs pubescent; leaves more or less pubescent 5
5. Base of leaflets usually truncate or rounded, asymmetrical;
  upper surface dark yellow-green, soft-pubescent beneath . . . .
. . . . *F. tomentosa* Michx. f. (*F. profunda* Bush) (Pumpkin ash)
5. Base of leaflets usually acute; leaflets 5–9, elliptic-
  lanceolate . . . . *F. pennsylvanica* Marsh. (Red ash)

GINKGO BILOBA L. (Maidenhair tree, ginkgo)

Gleditsia
1. Pods 2–4 dm. long; trees of various sites . . . .
. . . . *G. triacanthos* L. (Honey locust)
1. Pods less than one dm. long; trees restricted to bayou banks
  or river bottoms . . . . *G. aquatica* Marsh. (Water locust)

Gymnocladus dioica (L.) K. Koch (Kentucky coffee-tree)

Halesia carolina L. (Silverbell, peawood)

Hamamelis virginiana L. (Witch hazel)

Ilex
1. Leaves evergreen . . . . *I. opaca* Soland. in Ait. (American holly)
1. Leaves deciduous 2
   2. Leaves cuneate, obtusely serrate or crenate . . . .
. . . . I. decidua Walt. (Deciduous holly)
   2. Leaves seldom cuneate, sharply serrate 3
3. Buds spreading, blunt; nutlets smooth; swamps and low woods . . . .
. . . . I. verticillata (L.) A. Gray (Winterberry, black alder)
3. Buds appressed, pointed; nutlets ribbed or striate; trees of
  well-drained sites 4
   4. Leaves essentially glabrous . . . .
. . . . *I. montana* Torr. & Gray (*I. monticola* A. Gray) (Mountain holly)
   4. Leaves downy beneath . . . .
. . . . *I. montana* var. *mollis* (Gray) Britt. (Hairy mountain holly)

Juglans
1. Pith chocolate-colored; leaf-scars with a downy cross-line at top, not notched; fruit longer than broad, hull sticky-glandular.......................... ... *J. cinerea* L. (Butternut)
1. Pith tan; leaf-scars without a downy ridge at top, notched; fruit essentially spheroidal, hull not glandular.......................
   J. nigra L. (Black walnut)

Juniperus virginiana L. (Red cedar)

Kalmia latifolia L. (Mountain laurel, "ivy")

LIGUSTRUM VULGARE L. (Privet)

Lindera benzoin (L.) Blume (Spicebush)

Liquidambar styraciflua L. (Sweet gum)

Liriodendron tulipifera L. (Tulip tree, yellow poplar)

MACLURA POMIFERA (Raf.) Schneid. (Osage orange, hedge-apple, bois d'arc)

Magnolia
1. Leaves deciduous................ 3
1. Leaves evergreen.. 2
   2. Leaves averaging more than 7 cm. broad, leathery, persistent, usually rusty tomentose beneath........................
   .... M. GRANDIFLORA L. (Evergreen magnolia)
   2. Leaves averaging less than 7 cm. broad, thin and semi-persistent, pale or nearly white beneath................. ....
   .... *M. virginiana* L. (Sweet bay)
3. Leaves cordate at the base........................... 5
3. Leaves not cordate at the base....................... 4
   4. Leaves 1.5-2.5 dm. long........... *M. acuminata* L. (Cucumber tree)
   4. Leaves 4.5-5 dm. long.......... *M. tripetala* L. (Umbrella magnolia)
5. Leaves strongly auriculate, not whitened beneath, 2.5-3 dm. long; petals 2.5-4 dm. long........ *M. fraseri* Walt. (Mountain magnolia)
5. Leaves not strongly auriculate, pale to nearly white beneath, 5-7.5 dm. long; petals 1.5 dm. long........ ....
   .... M. macrophylla Michx. (Large-leaved magnolia)

Morus
1. Leaves harsh above, more or less tomentose below, infrequently lobed.......................... *M. rubra* L. (Red mulberry)
1. Leaves smooth on both sides, usually lobed........................ 2
   2. Fruit white....................... *M. ALBA L. (White mulberry)
   2. Fruit red to purple...
   .... M. ALBA var. TATARICA (L.) Ser. (Russian mulberry)

Nyssa
1. Leaves of fertile branches 10–30 cm. long; fertile flowers
   solitary; fruits 2–3 cm. long . . . . *N. aquatica* L. (Tupelo)
1. Leaves of fertile branches 2.5–15 cm. long; fertile flowers
   2 or more on each peduncle; fruits less than 1.5 cm. long 2
   2. Winter buds 3 mm. long; leaves often glaucous below;
      stone of fruit conspicuously ribbed . . . .
      . . . . *N. sylvatica* var. *biflora* (Walt.) Sarg. (Swamp black gum)
   2. Winter buds 6 mm. long; leaves not glaucous below; stone
      of fruit indistinctly ribbed . . . . *N. sylvatica* Marsh. (Black gum)

Ostrya virginiana (Mill.) K. Koch (Hop hornbeam, ironwood)

Oxydendrum arboreum (L.) DC. (Sourwood)

PAULOWNIA TOMENTOSA (Thunb.) Steud. (Empress tree)

Picea rubens Sarg. (Red spruce)

Pieris floribunda (Pursh) B. & H. (Rosemary, fetterbush)

Pinus
1. Leaves characteristically 5 in a bundle . . . .
   . . . . *P. strobus* L. (Eastern white pine)
1. Leaves 2 or 3 in a bundle 2
   2. Leaves characteristically 2 in a bundle; or in both twos
      and threes 4
   2. Leaves characteristically 3 in a bundle 3
3. Leaves 15 cm. long or more; cones 7–15 cm. long . . . .
   . . . . P. taeda L. (Loblolly pine)
3. Leaves 7–13 cm. long; cones 5–8 cm. long . . . .
   . . . . *P. rigida* Mill. (Pitch pine)
   4. Cones commonly asymmetrical, often more than 7 cm. in
      length, with very stout prickles . . . .
      . . . . *P. pungens* Lamb. (Table mountain pine)
   4. Cones usually symmetrical, with slender prickles, less
      than 7 cm. in length 5
5. Branches nearly smooth; leaves twisted, usually less than
   5 cm. long, in twos . . . . *P. virginiana* Mill. (Virginia pine, scrub pine)
5. Branches scaly; leaves not twisted, usually 7–13 cm. long,
   usually in both twos and threes . . . . *P. echinata* Mill. (Shortleaf pine)

Planera aquatica (Walt.) Gmelin (Planer tree, water elm)

Platanus occidentalis L. (Sycamore)

Populus
1. Fastigiate (with upright branches) . . . .
   . . . . *P. NIGRA* var. *ITALICA* Muench. (Lombardy poplar)
1. Not fastigiate 2

2. Petioles round; blade often 1.5 dm. or more long. . . . .
. . . . *P. heterophylla* L. (Swamp cottonwood)
2. Petioles flattened; blade smaller. 3
3. Teeth small, more than 14 on each side. 5
3. Teeth large, less than 14 on each side of the leaf-blade. 4
    4. Petioles averaging over 5 cm. in length; twigs and leaves
    essentially glabrous. . . . .
    . . . . *P. grandidentata* Michx. (Large-toothed aspen)
    4. Petioles averaging less than 5 cm.; twigs and leaves white
    tomentose. . . . . *P. ALBA L. (Silver poplar)
5. Petioles smooth. . . . .
. . . . *P. deltoides* Bartr. (Carolina poplar, cottonwood)
5. Petioles hairy. . . . . X P. GILEADENSIS Rouleau (Balm-of-Gilead)

Prunus
(A difficult group when without fruit and flower characters)
1. Terminal-bud typically present. 6
1. Terminal-bud typically absent, represented by a scar. 2
    2. Buds elongate, longer than thick. 4
    2. Buds scarcely longer than thick. 3
3. Leaves usually 6–10 cm. long; calyx lobes glandular. . . . .
. . . . *P. munsoniana* Wight & Hedrick (Munson plum)
3. Leaves mostly 2–6 cm. long; calyx lobes without glands. . . . .
. . . . *P. angustifolia* Marsh. (Chickasaw plum)
    4. Leaves thin, lustrous, acute or acuminate, crenate-dentate. . . . .
    . . . . *P. hortulana* Bailey (Wildgoose plum)
    4. Leaves dull, dark green, abruptly pointed at apex, sharply
    serrate. 5
5. Trees forming thickets from root-sprouts; leaves acuminate
from the first. . . . . *P. americana* Marsh. (Wild plum)
5. Trees without rootsprouts; leaves somewhat obtuse when they
unfold. . . . . *P. mexicana* Wats. (Big-tree plum)
    6. Twigs green or red. . . . . *P. PERSICA (L.) Batsch. (Peach)
    6. Twigs reddish-brown or gray. 7
7. Buds averaging 4 mm. long; flowers in elongate racemes. . . . .
. . . . *P. serotina* Ehrh. (Wild black cherry)
7. Buds averaging either shorter or longer; flowers not in elongate
racemes. 8
    8. Buds 3 mm. long or less. 10
    8. Buds 5–7 mm. long (escaped, edible cherries). 9
9. Buds glossy, ovoid-fusiform. . . . . *P. AVIUM L. (Sweet cherry)
9. Buds duller or darker, round-ovoid. . . . . . . *P. CERASUS L. (Sour cherry)
    10. Leaves incurved-crenulate, reaching 1.5 dm. long; fruit
    bright red; tree of high mountains, common in openings
    and after fire. . . . . *P. pensylvanica* L. f. (Fire cherry, pin cherry)
    10. Leaves finely and sharply serrate with glandular teeth,
    not reaching 1 dm. long; fruit dark reddish-purple; trees
    of lower altitudes. . . . . *P. alleghaniensis* Porter (Allegheny plum)

Pyrus (including *Malus*)

1. Leaves oblong-ovate, hard and shiny, with crenate-serrate margins; buds glabrous, conical; escaped forms often with spinose branchlets........................ *P. COMMUNIS L. (Pear)
1. Leaves ovate to lanceolate, with prominent teeth or lobes, or persistently woolly beneath................................. 2
   2. Branches without thorns; buds pubescent; leaves hairy or woolly beneath.......................... *P. MALUS L. (Apple)
   2. Branches usually armed with hard, sharp lateral spurs.............. 3
3. Leaves on vigorous shoots pubescent below at maturity...............
.... *P. coronaria* var. *lancifolia* (Rehd.) Fern. *(M. bracteata* Rehd.) (Lance-leaved crab)
3. All leaves glabrous at maturity.................................... 4
   4. Leaves usually less than twice as long as broad, frequently lobed, leaves on flowering branches acute or acuminate.............
.... *P. coronaria* L. (Sweet crabapple)
   4. Leaves usually more than twice as long as broad, unlobed leaves on flowering branches obtuse..... ....
.... *P. angustifolia* Ait. (Narrow-leaf crabapple)

*MELIA AZEDARACH L. (Chinaberry)

Quercus

1. Leaves characteristically lobed, toothed, or both..................... 6
1. Leaves characteristically entire (unlobed and untoothed).............. 2
   2. Leaves rhomboidal, widest above the middle......................
.... *Q. nigra* L. (Water oak)
   2. Leaves widest near the middle, tapering gradually toward both ends.. 3
3. Leaves evergreen, persisting throughout the winter, without bristle tips; margins revolute.......... *Q. VIRGINIANA* Mill. (Live oak)
3. Leaves deciduous, with bristle tips................................ 4
   4. Leaves over 2.5 cm. wide, 3 times as long as broad, often hairy below..................... *Q. imbricaria* Michx. (Shingle oak)
   4. Leaves typically less than 2.5 cm. wide......................... 5
5. Leaves typically narrowly lanceolate, deciduous in the fall.............
.... *Q. phellos* L. (Willow oak)
5. Leaves typically elliptical, margins slightly revolute, deciduous in late winter.................... *Q. laurifolia* Michx. (Laurel oak)
   6. Leaves broadest near the tip (about 1/6-1/4 from the apex); not conspicuously lobed or toothed........................... 7
   6. Leaves broadest nearer the middle, with conspicuous teeth or lobes.. 8
7. Leaves 1-1.5 dm. long, lower surface brownish scurfy, round or cordate at base.............. *Q. marilandica* Muench. (Blackjack oak)
7. Leaves .5-1 dm. long, lower surface smooth and shining, tapering to the base............................. *Q. nigra* L. (Water oak)
   8. Leaves distinctly lobed....................................... 12
   8. Leaves with coarse teeth or scalloped but not distinctly lobed... 9
9. Teeth acute.................. *Q. muehlenbergii* Engelm. (Chinquapin oak)
9. Teeth rounded or margins scalloped............................. 10

10. Leaves coarsely sinuate-toothed or with irregular
shallow lobes, usually with 6-8 pairs of lateral veins,
not all ending in teeth; acorns on stalks 5-10 cm. long.............
.... *Q. bicolor* Willd. (Swamp white oak)
  10. Leaves mostly with more than 9 pairs of lateral veins,
  all ending in regular teeth; acorns short-stalked................. 11
11. Petioles yellowish; leaves yellow-green above, pubescent
but not tomentose beneath; trees of dry uplands (to 5,000 ft.)...........
            Q. prinus L. *(Q. montana* Willd.) (Chestnut oak, mountain oak)
11. Petioles green; leaves dark-green above, commonly tomentose
beneath; trees of lowlands and wet soils............................
.... *Q. michauxii* Nutt. (Swamp chestnut oak)
  12. Lobes of leaves with bristle-tips............................... 16
  12. Lobes of leaves without bristle-tips........................... 13
13. Leaves glaucous and glabrous beneath at maturity..................
.... *Q. alba* L. (White oak)
13. Leaves densely gray-pubescent beneath........................... 14
  14. Twigs pubescent; leaves generally with 5 principal lobes;
  acorns small, 1-1.5 cm. long, less than half covered by the
  unfringed cup...................... *Q. stellata* Wang. (Post oak)
  14. Twigs glabrous or nearly so; acorns more than half covered
  by the cup... 15
15. Acorn cup conspicuously fringed along margin; acorns 2-5 cm.
long; leaves nearly cut in two by deep sinuses.....................
.... *Q. macrocarpa* Michx. (Bur oak)
15. Acorn cup not fringed, nearly covering acorn, which is 1.5-
2.5 cm. long; leaves irregularly lobed........ *Q. lyrata* Walt. (Overcup oak)
  16. Mature leaves smooth beneath except for tufts of hairs
  in the major vein-axils..................................... 19
  16. Mature leaves more or less pubescent on the whole under
  surface... 17
17. Leaves brownish or rusty pubescent beneath, lobes not
curved, frequently wider toward the end...........................
.... *Q. velutina* Lam. (Black oak)
17. Leaves grayish or yellowish pubescent beneath, lobes
generally curved and widest at the base.......................... 18
  18. Leaves variable in shape, mostly 3-5 lobed, some with a
  long slender central lobe......................................
  .... *Q. falcata* Michx. (Southern red oak)
  18. Leaves more uniform in shape, mostly 7-11 lobed, with
  the upper edges of lobes almost perpendicular to the mid-
  rib..
          Q. falcata var. *pagodaefolia* Ell. (Swamp red oak, cherrybark oak)
19. Lateral lobes of leaves not decidedly longer than the width of
the undivided portion of the blade; leaves dull, 7-11 lobed;
acorn cup saucerlike...
............./....... *Q. rubra* L. *(Q. borealis* Michx. f.) (Northern red oak)
19. Lateral lobes of leaves decidedly longer than the width of the
undivided portion of the blade; leaves lustrous, 5-9 lobed............. 20

20. Acorn cup saucerlike, seldom enclosing more than one-
fourth of the acorn.......................... 22
20. Acorn cup bowl-shaped, enclosing almost half of the
acorn.. 21
21. Acorn with several concentric rings near apex, 1.5-2.5 cm.
long and about as broad; upland sites, usually dry....................
.... *Q. coccinea* Muench. (Scarlet oak)
21. Acorn without concentric apical rings, 2-3 cm. long, longer
than broad; bottomland sites.......... *Q. nuttallii* Palmer (Nuttall oak)
22. Acorn oblong-ovoid, 2-3 cm. long; limestone sites...............
.... *Q. shumardii* Buckl. (Shumard red oak)
22. Acorn hemispherical, 1-1.5 cm. long; branches like pins
driven into trunk, frequently drooping; bottomlands or upland swamps...................... *Q. palustris* Muench. (Pin oak)

Rhamnus caroliniana Walt. (Carolina buckthorn)

Rhododendron
1. Leaf-blades about 3.5 times as long as broad, tapering at
base, green to brownish beneath.......... *R. maximum* L. (Great laurel)
1. Leaf-blades about 2 times as long as broad, rounded at base,
whitish beneath.................... *R. catawbiense* Michx. (Rose bay)

Rhus
1. Leaf scars U-shaped; rachis winged........ *R. copallina* L. (Dwarf sumac)
1. Leaf scars C-shaped or broadly crescent-shaped; rachis not
winged.. 2
2. Leaflets entire (POISONOUS)........... *R. vernix* L. (Poison sumac)
2. Leaflets serrate... 3
3. Stems glabrous or nearly so; twigs often 3-sided...................
.... *R. glabra* L. (Smooth sumac)
3. Stems hairy, concealing the lenticels; twigs rounded.................
.... *R. typhina* L. (Staghorn sumac)

Robinia
1. Branches with short, stiff, paired, stipular thorns; twigs
and petioles not sticky................. *R. pseudoacacia* L. (Black locust)
1. Branches usually without stipular thorns; twigs and petioles
very sticky.......................... *R. viscosa* Vent. (Clammy locust)

Salix
1. Branchlets strongly drooping.......................................
.... *S. BABYLONICA* L. (Weeping willow)
1. Branchlets not strongly drooping................................. 2
2. Leaves whitish beneath................. *S. ALBA* L. (White willow)
2. Leaves green beneath....................................... 3
3. Leaves closely and finely toothed; petioles distinct....................
.... *S. nigra* Marsh. (Black willow)
3. Leaves distantly toothed, nearly sessile...........................
.... *S. interior* Rowlee *(S. longifolia* Muhl.) (Sandbar willow)

Sassafras albidum (Nutt.) Nees (Sassafras)

Sorbus americana Marsh. *(Pyrus americana* (Marsh.) DC.) (Mountain ash)

Stewartia ovata (Cav.) Weatherby (Mountain stewartia)

Symplocos tinctoria (L.) L'Her. (Sweetleaf, horse sugar)

Taxodium distichum (L.) Rich. (Bald cypress)

Thuja occidentalis L. (Northern white cedar, arbor vitae)

Tilia

  1. Lower surface of leaves pubescent or felted-tomentose 3
  1. Lower surface of mature leaves glabrous except for axillary
     tufts of hairs 2
    2. Introduced trees with leaf-blades averaging less than 8 cm.
      long . . . . T. CORDATA Mill. (European basswood)
    2. Native trees with leaf-blades averaging more than 10 cm.
      long . . . . *T. americana* L. (Basswood)
  3. Lower surfaces of leaves green, with scattered stellate or
    loosely enmeshed hairs . . . . *T. neglecta* Spach (Basswood)
  3. Lower surfaces whitened with felt-like or crowded and
    stellate pubescence. . . . . *T. heterophylla* Vent. (White basswood)

Tsuga

  1. Leaves extending more or less in one plane, averaging less
    than 1 cm. long; cones 1-2 cm. long; common tree of mountain
    valleys . . . . *T. canadensis* (L.) Carr. (Eastern hemlock)
  1. Leaves radiate, averaging more than 1 cm. long; cones 2-4 cm.
    long; rare tree of mountain ridges . . . .
    . . . . *T. caroliniana* Engelm. (Carolina hemlock)

Ulmus

  1. Leaves usually more than 7 cm. long 4
  1. Leaves mostly less than 7 cm. long 2
    2. Trees usually small; twigs wingless, dark gray; leaves
      singly serrate or nearly so . . . . U. PUMILA L. (Chinese elm)
    2. Trees often large; usually with twigs two-winged, reddish
      brown 3
  3. Leaves acuminate, coarsely doubly toothed, smooth above
    and hairy below; spring flowering . . . . *U. alata* Michx. (Winged elm)
  3. Leaves rounded or acute at apex, almost singly toothed, rough
    above and hairy below; fall flowering . . . .
    . . . . *U. crassifolia* Nutt. (Cedar elm)
    4. Branches with corky ridges 6
    4. Branches without corky ridges 5
  5. Bud-scales coated with rusty hairs; leaves very rough above;
    pedicels short; fruit not ciliate; inner bark mucilaginous . . . .
    . . . . *U. rubra* Muhl. *(U. fulva* Michx.) (Slippery elm)

5. Bud-scales without rusty hairs; leaves relatively smooth above; pedicels slender, drooping; fruit ciliate; inner bark not muci-laginous. . . . . *U. americana* L. (American elm)
   6. Bud-scales puberulent; spring-flowering. . . . .
   . . . . *U. thomasi* Sarg. (*U. racemosa* Thomas) (Cork elm)
   6. Bud-scales glabrous; fall-flowering. . . . .
   . . . . *U. serotina* Sarg. (September elm)

Vaccinium arboreum Marsh. (Farkleberry, winter huckleberry)

Viburnum
1. Leaves entire. . . . .
. . . . *V. nudum* L. (Large withe-rod, possum-haw viburnum)
1. Leaves minutely toothed. 2
   2. Buds short and broad, dark red-scurfy. . . . .
   . . . . *V. rufidulum* Raf. (Blue haw, rusty black haw)
   2. Buds long and slender, gray or reddish-brown. 3
3. Petioles winged; buds gray; branches limber. . . . .
. . . . *V. lentago* L. (Nannyberry)
3. Petioles wingless; buds reddish; branches stiff. . . . .
. . . . *V. prunifolium* L. (Black haw)

Xanthoxylum americanum Mill. (Prickly ash)

DESCRIPTIVE LEAF TERMS

A. LEAF ARRANGEMENTS
   1. *Alternate.* Leaves borne one at a node in a spiral arrangement.
   2. *Opposite.* Leaves borne two at a node on opposite sides of the stem.
   3. *Whorled* (verticillate). Leaves borne three or more at a node.
B. LEAF PARTS
   One or more of the parts listed below may be absent or modified. For example, a sessile leaf is one which lacks a petiole. Stipules are fre-quently absent or modified.
   1. *Blade.* The major portion of the leaf, which is usually flat and ex-panded.
   2. *Petiole.* The stalk-like connection between the blade and the stem.
   3. *Pulvinus.* Thickened portion of petiole at base of leaf, blade or leaflet, characteristic of legume family.
   4. *Rachis.* The continuation of the petiole as the axis of a pinnately compound leaf. *Rachilla:* a secondary rachis.
   5. *Stipule.* One of a pair of small leaf-like appendages borne near the base of the petiole. Stipules may be modified into hairs, thorns, glands, etc.
C. LEAF SHAPES
   Leaves are usually bilaterally symmetrical. However, asymmetrical modifications of the following types also occur.
   1. *Cordate.* Heart-shaped.
   2. *Elliptical.* Broadest in the middle; having the form of an ellipse.

3. *Lanceolate.* Broadest near the base; lance-shaped.
4. *Linear.* Narrow form with more or less parallel sides.
5. *Needle-shaped* (acicular). Slender, hard leaves characteristic of pines and their relatives.
6. *Obovate.* Egg-shaped in outline; broadest above the middle.
7. *Orbicular.* Round in outline.
8. *Ovate.* Egg-shaped in outline; broadest below the middle.
9. *Scale-like.* Minute, appressed, triangular or ovate form characteristic of certain evergreens.
10. *Spatulate.* Narrow obovate form; broadest near the tip.
11. *Triangular* (deltoid). Three-sided form, either narrow or broad.

D. LEAF SEGMENTATIONS
1. *Simple.* A form in which the blade is not divided into leaflets.
   a. *Undivided.*
   b. *Pinnatifid.* Form in which the blade is variously divided into lobes and sinuses (a sinus is the notch between lobes), but not into separate leaflets.
   c. *Lobed.* Blade divisions with rounded sinuses.
   d. *Incised.* With shallow, irregular, more or less sharp divisions.
   e. *Cleft.* Deeply cut with narrow sinuses.
2. *Compound.* Blade divided into leaflets.
   a. *Pinnate.* Leaflets arranged in two rows along the rachis.
   b. *Palmate.* Leaflets radiate from the end of the petiole.
3. *Decompound.* More than once pinnately divided.
   a. *Bipinnatifid.* With the leaflets pinnatifid.
   b. *Bipinnate.* With the leaflets divided to the rachilla.
   c. *Tripinnatifid.* With the secondary leaflets pinnatifid.
   d. *Tripinnate.* With the secondary leaflets divided to the rachilla.

E. LEAF MARGINS
1. *Ciliate.* Margins fringed with hairs.
2. *Entire.* With a continuous margin, not lobed or toothed.
3. *Gland-tipped.* Hairs or teeth gland-bearing.
4. *Sinuate.* Strongly wavy.
5. *Spinose.* Margins, lobes or teeth with hard, sharp projections.
6. *Toothed.* Small marginal lobes.
   a. *Crenate.* Margins scalloped. *Crenulate:* small crenations.
   b. *Dentate.* With the teeth directed outward, *i.e.,* with equal sides. *Denticulate:* small dentations.
   c. *Serrate.* With the teeth directed toward the apex, *i.e.,* with unequal sides. *Serrulate:* small serrations.
7. *Undulate.* Wavy.

F. LEAF APICES *(Apex,* singular)
1. *Acuminate.* Margins curving gradually into a long slender tip.
2. *Acute.* Straight margins meeting in a sharp well-defined angle.
3. *Cuspidate.* Terminating abruptly in a short bristle or spine.
4. *Emarginate.* With a shallow notch.
5. *Obtuse* (rounded). Blunt tipped.
6. *Truncate.* As if cut off at the end.

G. LEAF BASES
1. *Acuminate.* Margins tapering to the base.
2. *Acute.* Margins forming a sharp angle at the base.
3. *Auriculate.* With conspicuous, rounded basal lobes.

    4. *Cordate.* Heart-shaped at the base.

    5. *Cuneate.* Wedge-shaped at the base; an exaggerated form of the acute base.

    6. *Hastate.* With pointed, outwardly directed basal lobes.

    7. *Rounded.* Base of blade blunt, margins forming a continuous curve.

    8. *Sagittate.* With pointed, downwardly directed basal lobes.

    9. *Truncate.* As if cut off at the base.

H. LEAF VENATION

    1. *Parallel.* Conspicuous veins extending from the base to the apex of the leaf.

    2. *Reticulate.* Veins anastomosing to form a net. (a) *Pinnate.* Principal lateral veins diverging in a regular manner from the midvein. (b) *Palmate.* Three to several main veins radiating from the base of the blade.

    3. *Dichotomous.* Each vein forking at intervals into 2 smaller veins of equal size.

I. SPECIAL LEAF TEXTURES

    1. *Membranaceous.* Thin, papery blade.

    2. *Coriaceous.* Tough, leathery blade.

J. LEAF SURFACES

    1. *Dull.* Not shiny.

    2. *Glabrous.* Smooth, devoid of hairs or scales.

    3. *Glaucous.* With a whitish, waxy bloom which will rub off.

    4. *Hairy.* With various filamentous epidermal outgrowths.

       a. *Pubescent.* With short hairs.

          Puberulent. With minute hairs.

          Downy. Abundantly pubescent with soft, short hairs.

          Silky. With appressed, soft, straight pubescence.

       b. *Villous.* With long, soft hairs.

       c. *Tomentose.* With densely matted hairs.

       d. *Glandular.* With gland-tipped hairs.

    5. *Rugose.* Wrinkled.

    6. *Scabrous.* Rough to the touch.

    7. *Scaly.* With various non-filamentous, flattened, appressed, epidermal outgrowths.

    8. *Shiny* (lustrous). Glossy, bright, polished.

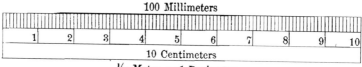

100 Millimeters

10 Centimeters

¹⁄₁₀ **Meter, or 1 Decimeter**